I AM...Inside of Me!

Publisher's Cataloging-in-Publication
(Provided by Quality Books, Inc.)

Penchina, Sharon.
I am-- inside of me! / by Sharon Penchina & Stuart Hoffman.
p. cm. -- (I am a lovable me! ; 5)
SUMMARY: Encourages children to protect and trust
their own sense of happiness, self-love and
self-confidence.
Audience: Ages 0-7.
LCCN 2006910391
ISBN-13: 978-0-9740684-9-7
ISBN-10: 0-9740684-9-7

1. Self-esteem in children--Juvenile literature.
2. Joy in children--Juvenile literature.
[1. Self-esteem. 2. Joy.]
I. Hoffman, Stuart, 1957- II. Title.

BF723.S3P463 2007   158.1'083
                                       QBI06-600709

Printed in China

I AM...inside of Me!

By Sharon Penchina C.Ht. & Dr. Stuart Hoffman

For Bev, with Love

2 Imagine
Scottsdale, Arizona
United States of America

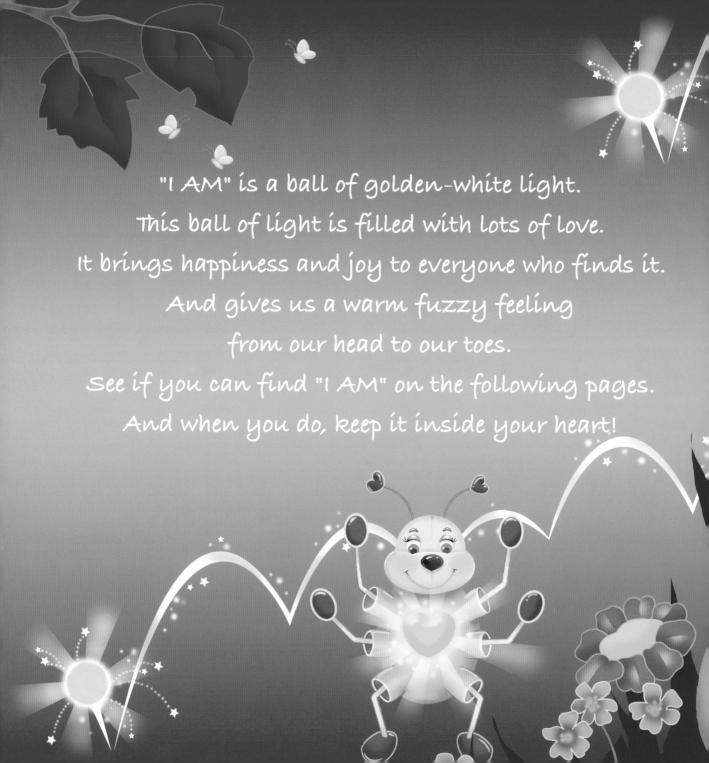

"I AM" is a ball of golden-white light.

This ball of light is filled with lots of love.

It brings happiness and joy to everyone who finds it.

And gives us a warm fuzzy feeling

from our head to our toes.

See if you can find "I AM" on the following pages.

And when you do, keep it inside your heart!

I AM...inside of Me!

Part 5 of the
I AM a Lovable ME!
Self-Empowerment series

Look within
and you will find where peace,
love and wisdom reside.

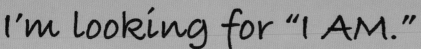

Or perched
in a tree?

Is it inside the house?

Has it gone to the park?

"I AM" might be right here, right here in the dark.

"I AM" has been misplaced.

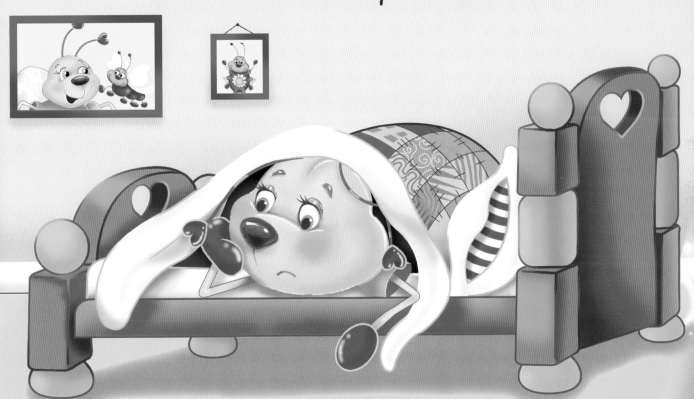

And, it's not in my bed.

I hope I can find it.

I've searched high and low.

And still I can't see

"I AM" hiding somewhere. Is it hiding from me?

I know if I'm
patient and I wait
its return,

"I AM" will come back

with some lessons I'll learn.

When I think of
"I AM" I will never
be blue.

Somewhere over there...
just out of sight.

"I AM" can be spotted
by its golden-white light.

I say the words, "I AM."
I SHOUT them loud
and clear!

And just then
it happens,
I know that it's near.

I stop and listen
as a voice seems to say,
"Love yourself and be loved,
more and more
everyday."

As light as a feather,

I float off
the ground.

I can now feel "I AM."

Here it is safe
and sound.

At last, I have found it.
"I AM" as pleased
as can be!
I will always remember,
that it's here...

...inside ME!